25000 Days

An Exploration

Anant Goswami

BookLeaf
Publishing

India | USA | UK

Made with ❤ on the BookLeaf Publishing Platform
www.bookleafpub.in
www.bookleafpub.com

Dedication

To family and friends,

And to you, dear reader.

Acknowledgements

I would like to thank my parents for giving me the gift of education and for tying me to a chair and forcing me to watch Rocky reruns on Star Movies back in the late '90s. I don't think I would have ever developed such a keen liking for the English language had I not witnessed Rocky Balboa exclaim – through a bloodied, swollen visage and in an equally slurred voice – 'Yo Adrian, we did it'! a thousand times.

I would like to thank my sister, Katyayani, because, well, inter-sibling diplomacy is a real thing.

I would also like to thank my friends, all of them, but some more equally than others (yes, an Animal Farm reference) for keeping me going through difficult times and offering tireless encouragement, even when I had thrown in the proverbial towel.

And last, but not least, I would like to thank Bookleaf Publishing for giving budding authors and poets a platform through which their deepest thoughts may be expressed to a wide, global audience. Thank you so much!

Preface

I'm sure you're wondering, 'Well, this is a seemingly innocuous and lithe little book about poetry – what does 25,000 days have to do with anything'? And to be honest, you're quite right to ask. Except that 25,000 days translates to the average human lifespan – give or take – and that's the closest I could come to completing the herculean task of tying together 21 disparate poems under a single common thread.

It's no secret that our time on this planet is limited, and I don't mean that in an Elon Musk-like 'We must leave Earth to colonise Mars' way. Without trying to sound too grandiose, I think we're all searching for answers, in one way or another.
One of the biggest questions that has bothered me, and shall always continue to do so, is the very nature of life itself.

These poems are, for the most part, a humble exploration of what makes us human. What inspires us? What do we fear? How do we cope with loss, trauma and the chaos of existence? And so on and so forth.

So, if you're someone who enjoys introspection and pondering the deeper questions of what makes us who we are, I wholeheartedly invite you to kick back and immerse yourself in these works. If nothing else, I hope these poems will serve as a starting point for your own dive into the vast oceans of why and how.

Index

Rage

He stands outside the
door,
Rapping with ferocity,
'It is I, Rage', exclaims
He,
'I am the purest'!
proclaims He,

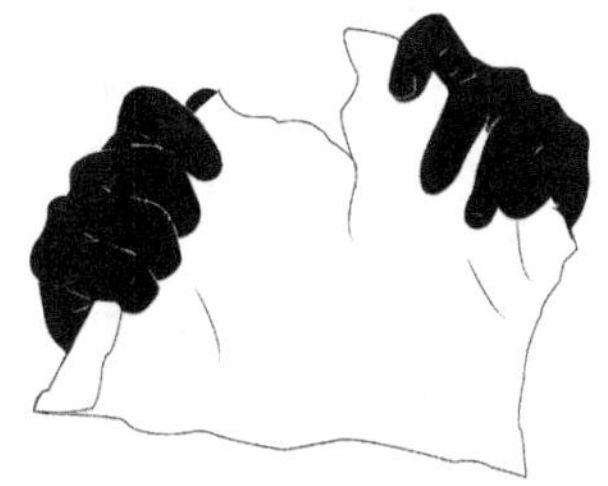

It is true; He is pure,
The purest, of all,
Not pervious to dilution,
Nor tempered by consideration,

He is Destruction,
As absolute as absolute,
A turn of the knob
And He shall enter,

A sweltering stellar furnace with atoms as
coal,
And hottest hellfire, satanic yet righteous,
But pale next to his frightening fury,
And yet, beware when He takes over,

For everything He touches is scorched,
Every word uttered, vile,
But it is you who must stand
In his wake of destruction,

It is you who must stand
When your crimes are arraigned,
Repentant and forlorn,
Your eyes wander the courtroom,

Looking for Him,
Don't. He is gone,
As sly as He was grand,

Choose wisely, O dear reader,
Hesitate, when He raps on that door again,
Choose wisely, O wise one,
Hesitate.

Espirit De Champion

What makes a champion?
We are humans,
Cold and logical,
Of course, the Fastest beats
Faster,

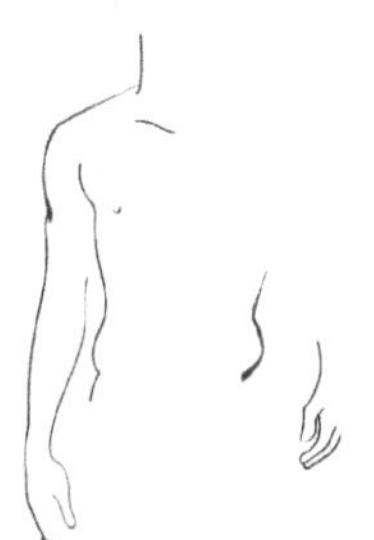

Who, in turn, beats the Fast,
And the champion is special,
There can only be one,
Without forgery or imitation,

Thus, though Fast and Faster
Are good and brave,
Fastest is the sole heir
To the Throne of Great,

So we take comfort in
This sweet hierarchy,
Unshakeable and unbroken,
But rudely, we are awakened,

You see, history is replete
With tales and legends

Of the meek beating the elite,
Goliath falling to David,

The Battle of Marathon,
Shocking Persian defeat,
And that war in Vietnam,
Humbling American retreat,

So Fastest can lose?!
But we are humans,
Shrewd and smart,
What then yields victory?

Is it guts? Or is it smarts?
Or does it lie deeper?
A fighting spirit?
A life-geist?

Indifferent to skill or luck,
It draws from beyond,
A realm within us
Deeply tucked,

But we are humans,
Neither gullible nor dumb,
Incredulous at such notions,
We scoff and mock!

And yet, the champion smiles,
Not of arrogance, but of wisdom,
She knows that neither numbers nor lines,
Predict all that may unfold,

When all seems lost,
When the darkest granite shrouds the sky,
And that demon before her,
Feeding on her deepest fears,

Roars in growing strength,
When her battered body cries, 'Stop'!
Every muscle, failing and numb,
Makes promises of pain yet to come,

Now, she draws upon it,
In her innermost recesses,
A strength unlike any other,
Latent, an anomaly,

Indebted to that inner spirit,
And with it, she is invincible,
As mythical as the demon himself,
And that is her victory,

Not of vapid ornaments,

Of gold, silver and bronze,
Desired by all, yet worthless
Without the crutch of validation,

But of wiping that debt,
To meet herself in the mirror,
In the eye each day,
And not look away – never look away.

The Last Stand

On a barren hilltop, on a
barren land,
Stood a fort of calcified
mud and rock,
Upon which stood
twenty-one men,
A swarm of ten thousand
closing in,

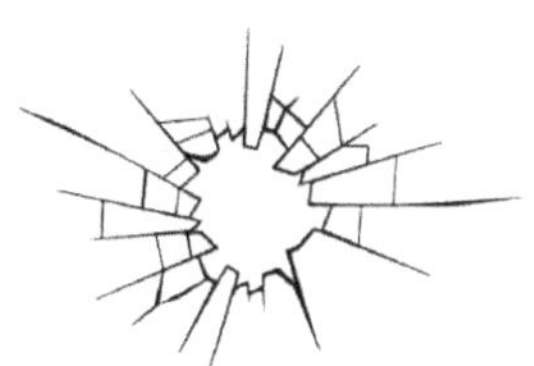

The choice was easy,
Defend the post and die,
Or retreat to live tomorrow, but they chose
Death,
Flipping that old choice the Reaper always
makes,

And then came the hoards,
The fort besieged by a tide
Of flesh, sweat and blood,
Metallic glints of swords,
Hung and flung at angles,
Flashed the tower-men blind,

And guns, cracking away,

A cacophony of off-pitched thunder,
Spewed seeds of death
At every pore of that rock tree,

Dust and debris dislodged around
The ducked tower-men,
Floating like wispy spirits,
Small deaths dancing in the sun,

The rock was their home,
And it too, would die

Then came the rumble,
That sickening thump of
Metal wasting wood,
The battering had begun,

Thump, crack, thump, crack,
Dust fairies waltzed with
Splinters ejected from the door
Thump, crack, thump, crack,
The tower-men rose and fired back,

Bam! Went down one invader,
Bam! Went down another,
Bam! This was no invader,
But the skull of a defender,

Red mist splashed out the back,
Spirit in tow, never to be captured,

And yet the Sun watched,
So did the mountain
And that wretched wasteland,
As the rock tree splintered
And flayed, strand after strand,

The defenders took note of the fallen
Yet continued on, their lips
In silent prayer
And triggers in the purest curse

At last, alas! Down came that door,
The tree fell, but the ground did shake,
Corpses festooned around the fortress,
So the bullets hadn't flown just one way,

A misty sprinkle against heavy rain,
The tower-men had done their all,
Death rushed through that dead door,
Vicious and vile, with steel teeth,
And gunpowder claws,

The defenders squared up to the beast,
A profusion of limbs and heads

Flew in that brutal melee,
Flowers torn by a petulant child,

One of the last few, a trembling teen,
Met the eye of the hive,
His resolve dissolving,
But then those ghostly words
Floated through that sick sky,

Sermons of his Guru,
Of doves fighting eagles,
The callow slashed through one,
Maimed another, and then came riposte,
Shiny steel tore through him,
What had hacked a teen now killed a man,

The messenger relayed on his trusty
heliograph,
Frenzied yet unerring, the tale of events
To beleaguered Lockhart and Gullistan,
Who with the Sun and mountain, watched
helpless

And then came a request to use his rifle
The messenger now stood last,
Armed with permission and benediction,
And his rusty breech-gun,

The messenger packed his heliograph,
And bolted his shed tight,

With parched throat and crusted lips
He aimed down his sight
Soaking earthen stairs crimson,
Till they set his shed alight,
As his skin peeled and mouth frothed,
He neither winced nor cried nor cowed,
But with one final bellow of his charred
lungs
Called his Guru aloud

And so concluded the brave stand,
Though they lost, yet they won,
For every hour that plagued Saragarhi
Blessed Lockhart and Gullistan,

Days later, regiments from the survivor pair
Reclaimed the ravaged fort,
'The Brave 21 of Saragarhi'
Would forever read History's report.

Adrift

I drift in this giant ocean
A plank keeping me afloat,
A remnant of the boat that
Sank some nights ago

Don't I belong with it?
Dead at the bottom of a dead sea
Why did it have to sink?
Why leave just me?

All I have is a pen and bottle,
Should I write my message?
And let capricious waves throttle
It to wherever they please,

Would it ever drift ashore?
Would anyone bother to read
Of my suffering, an epic of pointless pain,
That tired tale of futility?

I have become a drop of this ocean,
A wave rolling aimlessly,
No will, lost at sea,
Is this what was ordained?

O Fate, why give me a boat, then bury it
In Poseidon's darkest abyss?
Were it not gentler to end me on shore
Just before I set foot on wood?

For wicked Hope teases me as
I wobble and cry; mirages fly
Birds skip and scythe the horizon,
I am a prisoner to an open ocean.

Two Deaths

What happens when you
die?
Do you meet recalcitrant
black
Or recrudescent white?
Where are you, old friend?

Are you watching me
write?
A warm wraith stood
behind me,
Wispy fingers slipping into mine,
Typing each word as if it were your own,

Is there a heaven, or hell?
Where will I meet you?
For Gods are fickle, and
Abound within the follies of our mind,

Will I see you again, between this life and
the next?
Or never at all? It was good knowing you,

Though you may never see these lines,
I write them nevertheless,

We die two deaths, one when our heart
stops,
The other when we exist for no one,
The former is done, beyond my control,
The latter must wait till my own.

Duality of Hope

Hope is real, not abstract
Like arcane philosophy,
Or dead hypotheses,
Or whatever your fears
promise you,
It is as real as this book in your hand
And about as true,

But it's also not there if you think it's not,
Interstellar space, evening haze precluding
stars,
You standing on the sands of Mars,
A superposition of victory and defeat,
Think whatever of it; you are right,
Each time, and forever.

Loss

A tombstone bound to
your heart,
Sinking deeper through
you,
Into that fathomless sea of
bone and flesh.
You try to hack free, but
the braid fights back,
Growing thicker when it
should whittle,
It's bruising weight ripping your chest apart.

You throw in some slack, but it's futile,
For the respite is fleeting before searing
whiplash,
And your soul starts to fall asunder.
It is an endless riddle, not one of reason,
But of surrender – you must drown.
Therein lies salvation.

Wall of White

I stand in jittering cold,
My bones, frigid to the touch,
Before a wall of white that
Scales the sky, straddling the
horizon.

The peaks, piercing the heavens,
Snow-tipped spears of fierce legions.
An ocean of black rock suspended
In forever freefall, with droplets of
Houses clinging to ancient stone.

Yet in the shadows of these behemoths,
Fires burn and incense rises, as tiny feet
Scurry rocky paths at dawn,
Hands meet in prayer at dusk,
An homage to the great Himalayas.

Houses

Big or small, each house
tells a tale,
Of those who live
within,
And of itself – its birth
And impending death.

If you stray by the
façade long enough,
The rust on its metallic door,
Or the matted moss that sprawls its walls,
Speaks to you in hushed tones
Of the quiet lives that lie inside.

The windows, with criss-cross grills,
Break to you the glory days of past,
And the troubled hours of present, shrouded
By the walls of its proverbial prison.

And balconies, bathed in striated sunlight
That the loopholes let in, are lofty perches
Whence the residents might beam you
A half-smile or throw a curt stare.

There are myriad streets in the city,
And myriad houses in each of them.
A swath of stories to discover, yet we
Are trapped in one of them.

A Tryst by the Arabian
– I

One moonless
evening, a lad sits
anxious and giddy,
On a promenade by
the Arabian Sea. His
feet swing restlessly,
As he gazes into the
Stygian waters of a
canal,

Yellow lamps quivering off the water
Like the moons of Io and Calisto.

A destroyer sails into port, and his mind
drifts
To those waters under its hull, ones which
carried
Ancient Romans to lost Muziris some
hundred miles north,
Later welcoming Arabs and Europeans, all
alike.
But where are they now? Those brave
sailors stood upon

Braver vessels, chasing glory to the world's
edge?
Yet the waters remain, as steadfast as
The rock beneath his swinging feet,
It was a quarter to eight; where was she?

A Tryst by the Arabian – II

A gentle buzz draws him
from his mulling,
A familiar voice beckons him
to the end of the path.
His eyes scan those shades of
bright and dark.

Out she steps from the darkness into that
angelic yellow,
Shrouded in spectral amber, she squints,
Shielding bespectacled eyes with her palm,
That ethereal sight aching his ailing heart.
The two sit by a ledge, with black waters
below.

As a veiled Moon treks across the starless
sky,
The pair evoke Kipling, Longfellow and
Henley,
Of stoutness of hearts and never bowing the
head,
Of Gibran's warnings against half love.

She adores him, head rested upon shoulder
as
The golden beam against her glasses casts
fleeing shadows on her visage.
He gazes at her, etching all to memory,
Eyes curved into gentle crescents above
smiles, delicate creases round their corners,
Her mellifluous laughter and her eyebrows
slant like teardrops.
He looks at a wake in the water, foam
spreading thin into the black,
A thousand whispers on the Styx.
His exercise is futile, for when days grow
into years,
This memory shall slip
Like soft silt from clenched hands.

A Tryst by the Arabian – III

His gaze breaks upwards into
the dark horizon,
Thousands of miles away lies
Aden, Or Muscat,
Bathed in the dying embers of
the sun that drowned here hours
ago.
Yet the sun shall rise tomorrow, but this
moment shall fade.
Surviving only in the feeble sanctuary of
their minds,
Guarded against the torment of time till their
final breaths,
Vanishing into ether thence, forgotten like
those mariners of yore.
He looks back at her, into the black of her
eyes, a mind unburdened by knowing.
Envy claws at him.

The pair walk on a leafy pavement, the
pervading silence and solitude

Cut by the staccato thumps of feet meeting
concrete, reaching a
Grand old church, the ancient edifice shone
upon by that same ghostly yellow.
A lime yellow fenestration against the dead
of night.
She marvels at its majesty, while he
contemplates the history behind its great
doors.
Millions like them had stood before it, and
millions shall, praying for a life together.
His mind races through the many faces he'd
seen earlier, when he'd waited
Restlessly by the bank. Each pair was them,
but in a different tale,
Slipping away as quickly as they had
appeared, without a trace.

A Tryst by the Arabian – IV

He ponders the unyielding
will of the church,
The sea, and the stone
beneath his feet, dismissing
Those fleeting flashes of
love to their quiet funerals.
Not even a whispered note
in their timeless eulogies?
He beseeches those guardians to shed their
apathy,
To not let such beauty ebb away.
And what of the people themselves?
Lulled by the permanence of their quotidian
ways,
That bitter monotone ringing sweet with
repetition,
And what of the church and the sea, he
wonders?
For all their impassive arrogance, they too,
Shall dissolve to dust and vapour.

A glimmer of her golden necklace draws his
eyes,
Lying just above her heart, a tiny pendant
cross,
Its giant twin towering above the grand
church.
A faith not his own, a reminder of the
ceaseless divisions
Made on bodies of the same blood and soul.
Their story was doomed, crushed
Under the iron mallet of cruel dogma.
And alas! Came time to bid adieu,
He gazes one last time before turning north,
Imprinting her face onto the silver of his
memory,
Paths sealed forever in divergence.

Orion

If you were to gaze at the
stars
That bejewel the velvet
sky,
You wouldn't have to
look far
For a belt of three, frozen
mid-flight–
–Constellation Orion, the
hunter.

A raised arm of starry white,
Poised to strike, in eternal wait.
His gaze fixed on the edge of space,
On evil lurking in ghostly nebulae.

A silent sentinel, graven across
The endless canvas of time and space.

The Lonely Runner

In a ragged, decrepit
room
The burning glare of
television masks
The wrinkles on an
ancient face,
Who stares at a gaunt, lanky man
Running alone, towards him for hours.

The runner trots relentlessly as
The old man watches, still.
And the realisation hits–
He was the runner, furthest of all,
Yet the most forlorn,
The runner was not just him;
He was his nemesis: Time.

The old man sets on his own slow jog
Through the rundown lanes
Of fraying memory. He peers
Into alleys of years – some bad
Some good – but all his.
Faces of old friendships and
Failed loves wane in the demented fog,

Like drowning moons.

He crosses a boulevard of rendezvous
Straddled by dilapidated buildings,
Each tree a seed of passion sown decades
ago,
Whose fruits sprouted in tears down his
cheek.
With worn knees and hollowed heart
He rests by a bench, wondering where
They had all gone. For the runner's prize
was victory,
His was sinking solitude.

A Bench by the Bay – I

There lies a bench by the bay,
Huddled by the wall of a
resort.
Chipped concrete at the edges,
Rebar spine exposed
somewhere–
A battered relic like rocks by the sea.

A pair walk by, tired from a trek,
Friends or lovers, they do not know.
They rest on the salt-licked altar of grey,
And begin to gaze into the blue horizon,
Sun casting hues of neon orange
Playing its swansong on the other end.

The man remembers the resort from a
memory
Far ago, when he had barely aged past
twelve,
Chasing friends in the resort's green gardens
while
His parents smiled from the balcony above.

The memory writhes and mutates–
A haunting nightmare of a thousand
redheads,
In whose eyes the gardens charred black
And his parents lay eviscerated, limb for
limb.

The nightmare tears out of him, repressed
trauma
Choking his tongue as he struggles to
speak–
A stutter here, a stutter there
And a frequent squeak.
Dying rays of the sun wander
In the tears of moist eyes.

His companion meets his flooded gaze,
Shocked mum by the shift of emotion.
With careful steps of her weighted words,
She approaches the innermost bunker
Of his war-torn past, a child cowed
Next to a mortar shell that never blew.

The child, terrified of her presence,
Scrambles to the far end, bare skin
Against the cold comfort of concrete,
A shivering trigger in his outstretched arm.

A Bench by the Bay – II

The girl dares not move closer–
Only the warmth of her voice creeps ahead,
A glowing lull entombs the child.
His stare conflicted between the trigger and
her.

Her voice, a lullaby, promises him of worlds
Beyond the simmering fields under a red
sun–
Of quiet Elysian gardens with velvet flowers
And rivers glittering under a watchful sky.

He distrusts her – scabs ripped off painfully;
A mirage sold for a dream by snakes veiled
as seraphs.
Her promises ring hollow,
Echoes in a barren valley.

He points the barrel at her, squarely.
She steps back in a dignified retreat
Whence she came, leaving the bunker door
ajar.
The child, still stifled under the acrid air

Of his mind's grave, sees a string of light
Lace through those impregnable walls.
He feels the weight of the pistol,
Realising the burden he need not carry.

With trepid steps, he leaves the bunker,
And sees her standing in the distance–
A faint beacon of hope across a lifeless
desert.
He picks up his pace and marches on.

The man peers into the horizon,
As the last rays of the sun break
Across waters into a blackening sky.
Her words resound with resolve
In the placid chambers of his mind.
No garden shall ever burn again.

Better Not Know

Do you really want to know?
It is not the gift you think it
is.
To know everything that
shall ever happen.
And what fun is that?

To know your last day here.
Would it help if it were tomorrow?
Would it help if it were decades away?
Wouldn't you be saddened, all the same?

To know when every tragedy shall befall
you,
Or every raffle that you shall win.
Do you really want your victories
And defeats laid before you,
A tapestry of all there is?

To know every outcome of pitch and toss,
Or, how each story ends.
To miss Mystery's thrilling touch,
A life as white as a wall.

What good is an ocean without its waves?
A desert without its dunes?
It is better to wade in the dark
Than dawdle in the sun.

Flower of Jasenovac

It stood, an explosion frozen in
time,
Upheaved black against the
white of snow,
Brutalist petals reaching to
skies; arms of peace,
Sprawling from its slender
stem,
A monument unlike any other.

On its hollowed interior are etched
Names, hundreds of thousands,
Flowers that never came to bloom,
Lost to the pestilence of genocide.

A call to unity sprouting from
A bedrock cracked by division,
To honour it, not just with wreaths
But with change, so there may never
Grow another stone flower of Jasenovac.

Night

I walk across a still street
In the dead of the night,
A stare burns in the back
of my head,
I turn around; there is no
one.

The lane is empty,
houses with
Eyes bewitched in deep
sleep.
I see shadows swaying,
Melting in a witch's pot
On the precipice of streetlamps,
Jeering to cross over into the light.

Am I really alone?
Every step of my feet on
Cursed stone, feels like two,
A rustle in the shrub–
A bloodshot demon,
Or a twitching thug,
Possessed by their common lust
For money, an endless quest.

Or maybe it is just the thrill of claret
Seeping into dark earth, black,
Trickling into gutters of the underworld,
As my body twitches its eulogy.
I must hurry. The longer I stay,
The more powerful they get.

Life

If you are reading, you
are alive, and
You must realise – for
everyone today
Stand fifteen who lived
before us.
Fifteen souls stood
behind you,
Their ethereal faces contorting
Into a sheepish smile, as you weep
At the undulations of life.

The heady wisps of petrichor you breathe
On a rainy evening, or the orange rays
Of a setting sun blessing your vision,
Are luxuries they would give anything for:
To feel sand slip beneath your feet
On an azure beach of white and gold,
Or to even carry the burden of sorrow,
Their old friend, who never grows old.

As you, angry and wronged,
Kick a pebble down the road,

They reach out, spectral arms
Gliding through matter,
In futile reminder – you too will
Join us and realise the beauty of
All you leave behind.

So dear reader, fret not at life's vagaries,
Its petulant, childish whims,
For the woes are the price of luxuries
Those fifteen yearn to feel again.